LET'S TALK
ABOUT EASTER

by
Kathleen M. Clark

ISBN 0 86071 458 6

MOORLEY'S Print & Publishing

23 Park Rd., Ilkeston, Derbys DE7 5DA
Tel/Fax: (0115) 932 0643

Author's Note

These illustrations, stories and poems may be put together to form a Junior Church Service or used as part of Adult Worship.

Kathleen M. Clark as Head of Religious Education used them successfully in school assemblies and Youth Groups. She has had hundreds of poems and stories published in books, newspapers and magazines.

Dedication

For Connie - and friendship

The Meaning c

God so loved the world that He al
it. Real love has no boundaries, even i
It expects nothing in return and seeks

Christian love asks for total commitment. It is not like a Sunday suit which we can put on when we feel it expedient and take off when it limits our enjoyment. It is an everyday garment which we should wear with pride and humility.

In this modern world where pleasure is paramount, how often do we lift our eyes to the Cross of Calvary and marvel at the love which could endure such agony for our sakes? Does the gift of an Easter Egg ever remind us of the Resurrection - new life from the Tomb? - because that is what it is meant to represent.

The Easter Cross should mean that death loses its fear. The good we do in this life lives on after us in the lives of others. There is a sense in which that is our immortality. Our names may be forgotten but our unconscious influence lives on, perhaps in the eyes of a child alive because of some small forgotten act of generosity of ours.

We inherit a feeling of loving companionship without limits in good times and bad. I am sure the thief who spoke to Jesus as he was dying felt it, as have countless others through the ages.

The Cross negates useless regret and urges us to be the best we can within the light of our experience at any given time. It widens our vision and enables us to put past mistakes behind us and go forward in the light of this liberating knowledge. Boundaries cease to be barriers and become goals.

Even in His agony Jesus remembered to ask John to take care of His mother after His death, thus continuing the Jewish tradition of *'Honour thy father and thy mother....'* Suffering is not always a destroyer, it can heighten our sensitivity to the pain of others.

Easter reminds us that love triumphs over tragedy. It can never be killed so there is always hope. Real love will go to the uttermost. It scarifies, purifies and eventually heals those who commit themselves unreservedly to its service.

A Truth

'Ah', said the wise old minister to the distressed soul who had sought his counsel, 'We all have our Good Fridays. It may be the day you lose the one who is dearest to you, or when you discover your child is on drugs or when your best friend has let you down that you need your faith most. Perhaps a love that has never really been tested has a step further to go. Believe me, if you put your trust in God you will emerge stronger than ever to walk the Christian way. Go home and say your prayers and all will be well.'

Jesus Took A Donkey

Shaggy grey donkey
Of ancient fame
Derided by men
We cannot name.

Carrying the Master
How felt you then
Steadily bearing
The Lord of men?

Little grey donkey
Humble and meek
Yours was the honour
All Christians seek.

Let us then gently
Serve God and pray
We may meet Jesus
On Life's rough way.

Easter Events In Order

1. Jesus went to Gethsemane with three of His disciples to pray. They failed to keep awake as He asked them.

2. Men armed with swords and clubs arrested Him when He was betrayed by the kiss of Judas.

3. He was taken before the Sanhedrin - a Council made up of chief priests, scribes and elders.

4. They delivered Him to Pilate who was mystified by His answers to the usual questions.

5. Since He was a Galilean, Pilate passed Him over to Herod who likewise was not able to prove the allegations against Him.

6. Jesus was sent back to Pilate who again could find no case against Him. As was the custom at this time, he prepared to release one prisoner, but the crowd chose a murderer called Barabbas, thus relieving Pilate of the need to accuse Jesus of inciting the people to mutiny.

7. Jesus was sent to be crucified. A crown of thorns was placed on His head and the crowds spat on Him as He struggled on to Calvary.

8. Here He was crucified between two common thieves.

9. His body was placed in a sealed stone tomb given by Joseph of Arimathaea.

10. On Easter Sunday the tomb was empty. Jesus had risen from the dead.

The Crucifixion Cross

There seems to be no definitive record of the type of wood used to fashion the Cross on which our Lord was crucified. The fact that the same word was used for tree and wood adds to the difficulty.

If we turn to legends the choice is wider. In one area of Germany it was believed that the pear tree was used. It took root and eventually bore fruit which, when ripe, flushed red to remind men of the blood Jesus shed for them.

Much more widely known is the aspen whose leaves tremble all the time. Legend has it that they do so because it can never forget that its wood was used to make the Cross on which Jesus died. The same story is sometimes told about the poplar, a variation being that it trembles because it was the only tree which refused to mourn the Saviour's death. This it must regret for ever.

The elder is another tree which has become involved in the Easter story. There is a belief that this was the tree on which Judas Iscariot hanged himself because of his remorse for betraying his Master. Maybe this is why it is considered unlucky to burn elder wood in the house or use it to drive cattle to market.

I wonder if in years to come science will solve this mystery.

Word Derivations

Messiah - comes from a Hebrew word meaning the anointed. The Oxford Dictionary defines Him as the promised deliverer of the Jews.

Christ - means the anointed from the Greek for Messiah.

Jesus - comes from a Hebrew name meaning Jehovah saves or Jehovah is generous.

Remember This

The word Easter itself can form the basis of a talk or a children's address if we consider each letter and what it can stand for. Children will come up with many suggestions in response to a leading question e.g. What does everybody who is trying to lead a Christian life need first of all? I am sure you will get some surprising answers, but at least you have got your audience thinking.

E nthusiasm - The effort to stand up for Christian principles is often difficult but enthusiasm helps.

A ction - It is no use just being enthusiastic and doing nothing about it.

S haring - Why is it important to share our faith? When the going gets rough we need the support of others of like mind.

T emptation - What will spoil our efforts? Everyone, even Jesus, has to fight temptation. We must learn to say no to evil things like drugs.

E nergy - It is no good just sitting down and letting other people do the work.

R eliability - A Christian must never let other people down. He must keep his promises as Jesus did.

I would push the message home by using large cards. As each letter is dealt with the child bearing that card can stand in line. Sometimes the children would stand one behind the other or turn their backs and exchange cards. The audience is then asked what special word has been spelt and reminded finally of the importance of Easter.

Easter Monday At Hallaton - Leicestershire

The annual Hare Pie Scramble and Bottle-kicking at Hallaton is probably the best known of the Easter Monday revels. It was always regarded as a day for having fun and letting off high spirits.

The origins of the Scramble are lost in history although there is an idea that a hare saved a woman's life by diverting the attention of an aggressive bull as she was crossing a field. In gratitude she left the Vicar a piece of land if he would promise that hare pie, bread and ale should be scrambled for on the rising bank at the far end of the village.

The food and ale in three small barrels are taken in procession, complete with brass band, to a spot where a stream divides Hallaton from the next village. Here both teams try to kick the barrels into their own territory where the contents are polished off by the victors. A rugby scrum has nothing on the energy expended!

I often wonder if it reminds anybody in the excited crowd that but for our Lord's passion and death on the Cross the joy of Easter Monday would never have been ours.

Quotations

1. Christ has turned all our sunsets into dawns.
   - St. Clement of Alexandria.
2. Our Lord has written the promise of the Resurrection not in books alone, but in every leaf in Springtime. *Martin Luther.*
3. Easter says you can put Truth in a grave but it won't stay there. *Clarence W. Hull.*

The Legend Of The Poinsettia

A long time ago in a faraway land, a little boy wept because he wanted to join in the Easter procession to the local church, but to do so he needed a bunch of bright red flowers. He had been told that they represented Christ's blood shed on the Cross.

Although he searched for the whole morning, all he could find was a plant bearing pure white flowers but it had long powerful thorns. Still perhaps somebody would take pity on him and let him join in the celebrations, if he gathered a large enough bunch. As he picked the flowers, his little fingers became torn and bleeding but still he persisted until he could not hold any more.

As he stood up with tears in his eyes because of the pain in his hands, a tall man dressed all in white appeared at his side.

'Well done, little one,' said the stranger when the boy explained why he so much wanted to join the procession. *'I want to honour our Lord but I can't find any bright red flowers and I don't think these will do,'* he said piteously.

'Give me those blossoms', said the stranger and as He took them a strange thing happened. The thorns fell to the ground and the flowers slowly turned a bright red. *'Now,'* went on the stranger, *'You shall have your wish. I will banish the thorns and from now on the flowers of this plant shall be bright red to remind men of my Crucifixion and your faithfulness. Go now to your procession and be sure that I shall never forget you.'*

As the child looked down at the blood-red flowers in his hands he saw with amazement that his fingers were no longer bleeding and the flesh had healed miraculously.

He looked up again to thank the kind stranger, but He had vanished.

Easter Eggs

Even before Jesus was born, people gave eggs to one another to celebrate the return of Spring and new life after the dark days of Winter. It was the season of fertilisation and germination.

In pre Christian days, primitive people watched with wonder and amazement as new life burst from an object which on the outside looked, to them, like a stone. Later the emergence of this new life from the shell came to symbolise the Resurrection - new life bursting from the tomb.

Today the egg still plays a prominent part in Easter festivities and egg decoration is practised worldwide.

At Preston, Scarborough and other North Country places there are egg-rolling ceremonies. Brightly coloured, beautifully decorated eggs are rolled down suitable slopes. If the shell does not break the owner will have a year of good luck. It probably has more to do with the thickness of the shell and how hard-boiled it is than anything else. Some people think that the egg-rolling originally represented the stone being rolled away from Christ's tomb. This ceremony is also kept up at the White House in America.

In Yorkshire and Cheshire, the same custom but in a different form is kept up by the children on Easter Monday and is known as Pace-egging. Pace is derived from Paschal, meaning at Eastertide. The celebration takes the form of a play based on a sixteenth century text. The characters have strange names like Bold Slasher and Toss Pot. The latter always wears a top hat and carries a basket which was originally used to collect eggs from the spectators. Nowadays they collect money which is used as alms for the poor.

Midgely in Yorkshire is known for its Paschal drama performed by boys in brightly coloured tunics. They wear large, strangely decorated hats. Some also carry wooden swords. Unusually a large doll figures in the ceremony.

Edward I is said to have had four-hundred eggs boiled, stained or covered in gold leaf for his household. It is doubtful whether any of these were used in egg-rolling.

A custom which had all but died out but now seems to be enjoying a revival is the decorating of an egg tree. It is used as a room or table decoration according to its size, much as a Christmas tree is used at Yuletide. Ordinary eggs are blown and the contents made into custard etc. The shells are then dyed, painted or lavishly decorated with gold, silver or gilt paint. Often the colours used are those which denote the four elements: purple for earth, yellow for air, red for fire and blue for water. Sometimes small children are allowed to make figures of Pilate, Judas, etc. in dough. These are then baked hard and painted.

Most countries appear to have their own particular ways of giving or receiving eggs at Easter time. Some still reflect the fact that eggs were given a Christian significance when it became the practice to bring eggs, a forbidden food during Lent, to be blessed in church on Easter Sunday.

Similar games and contests are held in places which are far apart. For instance, in both N. England and Greece, hard-boiled eggs are used in a game where the egg is held sharp end on and knocked against the opponent's egg to test its strength. The one who scores the most hits without cracking the shell of his egg is declared the victor.

In one part of Germany, girls play a game where they are required to roll an egg through a special ring.

In Switzerland, a game is played where you try to beat your

Easter Biscuits Recipe

3 oz	butter or margarine	½ oz mixed peel (if liked)
2½ oz	caster sugar	2 drops of brandy essence
6 oz	self-raising flour	2 tablespoons of milk
2 oz	currants	½ teaspoon of mixed spice
1 egg separated		A little sugar
Pinch of salt		

1. Cream butter and sugar and beat in egg yolk.
2. Fold sieved flour, salt and fruit into this mixture.
3. Add spice, brandy essence and enough milk to make a soft dough.
4. Place in the fridge to become firm.
5. Knead lightly and roll out to ¼ inch thick. Cut out with 2 inch cutter.
6. Put on a baking tray and prick all over with a fork.
7. Bake for ten minutes at 200°C and then brush biscuits with egg white and sprinkle with sugar. Bake for a further 5-10 minutes at 180°/190°C.

———

Yorkshire Saying

On Good Friday rest thy pleaf (plough).
Start nowt, end nowt, that's eneaf (enough).

———

Inn Signs

Many of our inn signs mark the close connection between church and inn. For instance 'The Trip To Jerusalem' or 'Ye Olde Trippe To Jerusalem' as I have seen it written is a relic of the days when Crusaders passed through Nottingham and stopped at the castle on their way to join their King.

In a fictional context 'The Tabard' in Southwark was the inn where Chaucer's pilgrims in 'The Canterbury Tales' rested on their way to do homage at the shrine of Thomas a Becket.

So, although not specifically about Easter they are connected in a roundabout way with its events.

'The Lamb And Flag' is a much more definite allusion to the seasons events. People would rise early on Easter Sunday morning and go out to see what they believed to be the Lamb or the Lamb And Flag in the centre of the Sun's disc. Others had a firm belief, that survived from ancient times, they would see the sun dancing for joy on Easter morn in remembrance of Christ's Resurrection.

Easter and Weather Lore

The weather has always been of such crucial importance in the providing of food that it is no surprise to find many wise sayings connected with it. Here are a few of them.

1. Farmers look at rabbits to foretell what the winter will be like. A thick coat means a hard one, while a thin coat indicates that it will be mild.

2. The weather on Palm Sunday determines the prosperity of crops. A fine clear day indicates a good year for barley. This came from Finland.

3. In some parts of that country, people walk long distances on Easter morning to observe the sun. If it appears to dance in its tracks the year will be a prosperous one and if it rises in a clear sky the crops will be plentiful. A cloudy morning means poor crops and if the sun rises behind the clouds then the summer blossom can be killed by frost.

4. A rainbow at morn, put your hook in the corn.
    A rainbow at eve, put your hand on the sheave.

5. From an old nursery rhyme:
    If the wind on Easter Sunday is east, it is best to draw Easter water and bathe in it to prevent ill effects from the east wind throughout the remaining months of the year.

6. If the sun shines on Easter morning, it will shine until Whit Sunday.

7. A good deal of rain on Easter Day
    Gives a good crop of grass but little good hay.

8. If it rains on Good Friday and Easter Day
    There'll be plenty of grass and a little good hay.

9. If the sun shines on Easter Day, it will shine, if ever so little, every day during the year. If it rains there will be rain every day, although it may only be a few drops.

Easter Hymns

As is to be expected, some of our greatest and most popular hymns were written to celebrate Easter.

All Glory Laud And Honour which is usually sung on Palm Sunday was originally composed by St. Theodulph of Orleans who lived from 750 to 821. He was imprisoned for having allegedly taken part in the rebellion of the King's nephew against King Louis the Pious of France.

It is said that the King passed the prison in procession on Palm Sunday 821. Theodulph stood at the window of his cell and sang this hymn. It so impressed the King that he ordered Theodulph's release, gave him back his see and decreed that the hymn should be sung outside the prison every Palm Sunday.

Another version states that seven choirboys sang the hymn and so obtained the Saint's release. This used to be remembered at York and Hereford when seven choirboys were deputed to sing it in the Palm Sunday processions.

Charles Wesley (1707-88) wrote some 6,500 hymns in his lifetime. Even on his deathbed he dictated the last one to his wife.

Christ the Lord is risen today was probably written round about 1739 but left out of the Large Hymn Book published by his younger brother, John, in 1780. It lay undiscovered for many years before it was re-discovered in 1830 and became an integral part of Easter Christian worship worldwide.

My Faith Looks Up To Thee was the first hymn written by Dr. Palmer in 1830. It was published by Dr. Lowell Mason who wrote the tune Olivet in 1831. He told the author *'You may live many years and do many good things but I think you will be best known to posterity for this hymn.'* He has been proved right.

When I Survey The Wondrous Cross. The poet, Matthew Arnold thought this was the finest hymn in the English Language. He was even heard quoting it on the day of his sudden death.

George Eliot's aunt who was said to be the inspiration for the quick-tempered Methodist heroine in Adam Bede also recited lines from it on her deathbed. Countless other nameless people have been comforted by the beauty of its imagery.

<u>Jesus Lives</u>. This hymn was written by Christian Gellert (1715-69). He was a German Lutheran who had such a bad memory that he found preaching very difficult without the aid of extensive notes. Later he became a lecturer in Philosophy and was much beloved by his students.

His generosity was well-known. It is said that Prince Henry of Prussia found him living in one room without adequate food or heat. Poor he may have been but he has enriched many a Christian life with this hymn.

These are just a sample of some of the finest hymns ever written. Many more are worthy of our study.

Easter Time

Easter is the festival the Christian Church has chosen to represent the Resurrection.

Easter Sunday may not fall earlier than March 22nd or later than April 25th. It is fixed according to the date of the full moon following the Spring equinox.

Legends of Easter

The Lily Of The Valley

The legend tells how the broken-hearted Virgin Mary wept bitter tears at the foot of the Cross as Jesus was dying. These tears fell to the ground from whence sprung a pure white flower whose perfect small buds hung face downwards from slender green stems. They could not bear to look upwards and witness the agony of the dying Christ.

Larkspur

One of the most beautiful legends is said to have come from Asia. The Garden of Gethsemane was a lovely quiet place where many of the most attractive flowers and small animals could be found. After His death and the news of His Resurrection they all hoped Jesus would come and see them but for three days there was no sign of Him. When He appeared on the third day one little rabbit who had stayed awake day and night was rewarded with a loving smile. He smiled too on the larkspur lining His pathway.

Even now, it is believed, that if you look into the centre of each blossom you will see the image of the rabbit who waited so long and patiently to see the risen Jesus. There is a lesson here for everyone.

The Wild Rose

The Wild Rose is remembered because it is said that all its flowers were originally white. The story goes that when the Crown of Thorns was pressed down on the Saviour's head a drop of His blood fell on a nearby bush and ever after the flowers were either red or bordered with variations of that colour.

A Spring walk down an English country lane can still remind us of how Jesus suffered that we might have life and have it more abundantly.

The Primrose

One cold Spring day Jesus was walking down a country lane, alone and very sad because He knew His crucifixion was drawing near.

Suddenly He felt something warm touch His arm. It was a golden sunbeam who had been looking everywhere for Him. She wanted Him to know that she would do anything to ease His pain.

'Little one,' said Jesus, *'You have done that today. Rest now upon this bank where your beauty will never be forgotten and to remind men of your kindness you will flower each Spring. Goodbye Prime rose and thank you.'*

Nowadays in many country lanes in diverse countries the primrose blooms each Spring to remind us that however small and insignificant we are, we, too, can serve the Lord in our own way.

The Passion Flower

Although this is now a favourite house plant, it is a native of Brazil. The legend associated with it came from Mexico where it originated with a man called Jacomo Bosio. He said the bud was a symbol of the Holy Communion. As it opened, it looked like the Star which guided the Wise Men to the stable. The ten sepals and petals stood for the ten disciples at the Crucifixion and the five stamens reminded him of the five wounds inflicted on Christ's body as He died on the Cross.

The Iris

Thomas, the doubter, wanted to believe that Jesus would rise from the dead as He had promised but was finding it very hard. He was on his way to the Upper Room to meet the other disciples when he noticed a beautiful purple flower by the wayside. It sprung from a plant that weeks before he had noticed was withered and brown and had wished that he could revive it. Could this be a sign, he wondered, as he hurried on to find Jesus risen as he had promised. Now the iris reminds us of the Resurrection and its promise of life after death.

The Hawthorn

The legend of the two magpies does not seem to be at all well known. They were said to have covered Jesus with spiny hawthorn boughs to hide Him from the enemies who were trying to trap Him and take Him to be crucified.

From that time on the hawthorn has borne the fragrant white blossoms we know so well. These are followed by scarlet berries to remind us that its branches once protected Jesus when He was in great danger.

The Holy Thorn

It is said that this was brought to England by Joseph of Arimathaea when he was banished from the Holy Land and escaped to Glastonbury. Here he taught Christianity to the Britons.

His walking staff was a branch of the torn thorn tree and when he stuck it in the ground to mark the site of his new home, it put out leaves and flowered. It continued to do so for hundreds of years until it was destroyed by the Puritans.

A cutting believed to be from the original tree was planted in Washington D.C. and so the tradition lives on.

These are just a selection of the fascinating legends connected with Easter, so why don't you try and discover others?

Fact

A Staffordshire woman speaking in 1880 said that if a branch of hawthorn was gathered on Holy Thursday and kept in the house, that dwelling would never be struck by lightning because - Under a thorn our Saviour was born.

May Easter Day
To thy heart say
Christ died and rose for thee.

May Easter night
On thy heart write
O Christ, I live to Thee.

Anonymous.

Thoughts for Easter

If happiness is what we truly seek
We must not tread on other people's dreams
Or choose to think of tolerance as weak
For unearned fame is not the prize it seems.
If all we have to give - a helping hand
Then each new day's a very precious gift
Use it. Against unkindness make a stand
And you will feel your own low spirits lift.
We can achieve if we believe we can
With courage fight for what we know is right.
When we uphold the dignity of man
He will emerge from darkness into light.
If we want peace to fill the coming days
We must work hard to change our selfish ways.

Easter Quiz

1. It is possible for an adult to stand on an ordinary egg without breaking it. True or false?
    True.

2. What does the Easter greeting Christos Anesti mean?
    Christ is risen.

3. What is an Easter sepulchre?
    It is a canopied recess in a choir or chancel kept for the reception of the bread and wine consecrated on Maundy Thursday.

4. What do the letters A and O on the Paschal candle stand for?
    Alpha and Omega, first and last letters of the Greek alphabet.

5. What is the route Jesus was forced to walk to His execution, called?
    The Via Dolorosa.

6. What is Palm Sunday called in Spain?
    Pascua Florida, which means Flower Easter.

7. Which disciple refused to believe that Jesus had risen from the dead until he touched the wounds in His side and hands?
    Thomas.

8. Which American state got its name because it was discovered on Palm Sunday?
Florida.

9. Who do Spaniards sometimes call the Queen of Pain?
Mary, the mother of Jesus, because of what she suffered watching her son die on the Cross.

10. Where did Jesus live between Palm Sunday and Good Friday?
Bethany, a little village near Jerusalem.

11. Which day in Holy Week is the anniversary of the Last Supper?
Thursday.

12. Who created fabulous gold and precious stone Easter eggs for the Russian Royal family?
Peter Carl Fabergé, 1846-1920.

13. When is Hocktide?
It is the second Monday and Tuesday after Easter Sunday.

14. How was it celebrated?
Men and women were tripped up or bound to enforce payment of dues or the collection of money for churches and charities. It has long died out.

15. What were cramp rings?
Rings made from the handles of coffins were believed to be a protection against cramp and fits. This belief persisted well into the 19th century.

16. Who did the large doll sometimes placed on the top of an Easter bonfire represent?
Judas.

17. In which county are wells still dressed at Easter with religious pictures made from real flower petals embedded in clay?
Derbyshire.

18. According to ancient superstition, what was the hare supposed to do on Easter Eve?
Lay eggs for all good children.

19. Which of the disciples has a name meaning 'the twin'?
Thomas.

20. What were coloured Easter Eggs supposed to represent?
The return of flowers to the land after the bleakness of winter.

Hot Cross Buns

We think of them as exclusive to Easter but they actually date back to pre-Christian times. Pagan Greeks and Romans made small wheat flour cakes which were marked with a Cross and eaten at the feast of Diana.

Early Saxons ate similar small cakes as they worshipped the returning sun in March. Ancient Greeks offered such cakes to Astarte, the goddess of love and fruitfulness. Two petrified buns were found near Naples in an area destroyed by Vesuvius in 79AD.

There is a record that says similar cakes were given to the poor at St. Albans Abbey in 1361, but we do not know when the custom started there. Certainly by the 18th century it seems to have become popular everywhere.

In England, buns represented the unleaven bread Christ ate with His disciples in the Upper Room after signing them with a Cross.

As time went by, people believed that eating the buns was a cure for stomach ailments, dysentery, whooping cough and the like.

Gradually superstitions grew up around the custom. Some people believed that crosses made with a knife or with icing would keep evil spirits away from the place where they were made. Others averred that Hot Cross Buns baked on a Friday would stay fresh for a whole year, during which time the man of the house would not drown.

It was also believed that to hang a Hot Cross Bun from the ceiling would protect any building from bad luck or fire. In the last century some buns were hardened in the oven then hung until they needed to be grated and mixed with milk or water and given as medicine even to animals.

Bakers would work all night in order to be out selling them on the streets at dawn. There was intense rivalry to be first out. The most popular cry seems to have been:-

Hot Cross Buns!
One a penny, two a penny,
Hot Cross Buns.
If you have no daughters
Give them to your sons.
But if you have none
Of these merry little elves
Then me thinks you keep them
All to yourselves.

Easter Island

Easter Island was so named because Dutch Admiral, Roggeveen, discovered this lonely island on Easter Day 1722. It is a desolate place once used by Chile as a convict settlement.

It is saved from obscurity by 550 statues carved in the lava rock. The largest weighs over 100 tons and is 70 feet high. Some lie on their backs staring up at the sky. Some people believe that the island formed part of a great Pacific Empire which disappeared beneath the sea in the 17th century or thereabouts.

One opinion is that the first inhabitants were Maoris. The fact that all the statues have wide noses and nostrils as well as wide apart eyes seems to suggest that this is a possibility.

For All Who Care

I cannot put the world to rights
But I can play my part
And brighten my small corner up
The perfect place to start.
There I can treat folk kindly
Their joys and sorrows share
Help where I can by word and deed
To show I really care.

Prayers at Easter

1st Prayer

Oh God, when we watch the trees and flowers bursting into new life on this Easter morning, may it remind us of your promise of a more abundant life when we decide to follow the Christian path. Help us to walk with confidence in your footsteps. Amen.

2nd Prayer

Heavenly Father, we thank you that through the Resurrection we have a certain hope of Eternal Life. Take away from us the fear of Death and the sting of bereavement. Give us the strength to leave our loved ones in your peace, sure that they will forgive all our faults and misunderstandings even as you do. Amen.

3rd Prayer

Heavenly Father, we pray for all who suffer pain or deprivation. As we gaze up at the Cross, give us the strength to say of our enemies as Jesus did *'forgive them for they know not what they are doing to others'*. Help us to prove by our actions that we are doing our best to bring about the New World for which your son died on that cruel Cross at Calvary. As we rejoice in the beauty of the Springtime, grant that our minds remain open to the wonders of your Creation and thankful for our chance to play a part in it. Amen.

4th Prayer

Let us give thanks for the love that was willing to go even unto death. A love where no bitterness was attached. A love that could encompass Mary Magdalene and John, the beloved disciple, and which could see the value of a Mary and a Martha.

Oh God, give us the courage to be faithful when the going gets rough and if loneliness is our lot, teach us to rely on your presence in our lives. Keep us faithful to the best that is in us, strong in your strength to do the right and happy in the knowledge that underneath are the everlasting arms. Amen.

Resurrection Joy

With practised ease cold Winter strips each tree
And spoils its red-gold beauty with a sigh
As frosty light outlines its form we see
Black pencilled lace against a sullen sky.

Disgruntled rooks eye the bare branches here
And mourn the lack of shelter dolefully
Contented only when Spring buds appear
To lend the naked trees new mystery.

Still I see beauty in their Winter form
They sway and bend with free, uncluttered grace
Stand unabashed before a coming storm
Knowing that sun and warmth return apace.

So trees, like men, await upon Life's way
The glory of their Resurrection day.

An Easter Lesson

A young disabled man who wanted cheerful company not sympathy remarked, *'Yes, like the Easter Egg, I am encased in a hard, unyielding shell - but that does not mean that I lack a burgeoning, inner joy or that I shall be denied a glorious pain-free life after death. That's what the Easter story says to me.'*
Maybe we should all try to share that Easter message.

Easter Superstitions

CHRIST WAS CRUCIFIED ON A FRIDAY SO -

a)   It is bad luck to be born on that day.
b)   Adam and Eve were believed to have fallen from grace on that day.
c)   It is bad luck to cut your nails, change the bed, set sail or be sentenced to imprisonment.
d)   Country folk believed it was unlucky to knock nails in, shoe a horse or catch fish. Farmers would refuse to sell eggs on

Good Friday because they believed they were selling their good luck for that year.

e) On the Isle of Man it was considered unlucky to poke the fire with an iron poker so a stick of mountain ash was used instead.

f) If you did not eat a Hot Cross Bun on Good Friday your house would be burned down.

g) In some parts of Yorkshire it was believed to wash clothes on Good Friday was a sin. If they were hung out to dry they would be taken in spotted with blood, while in Berkshire in the 19th century some people believed that if washing was done on Good Friday the suds would turn to blood.

ON THE OTHER HAND -

a) A loaf baked on Good Friday was believed by other people to bring good luck and never go mouldy.

b) Seeds planted on Good Friday will produce a plentiful crop. Indeed, if you want parsley to flourish all the year round it should be planted on Good Friday.

c) Branches of ash placed round the door on Good Friday will keep out witches and evil spirits.

d) A child weaned on Good Friday will grow up healthy and strong.

e) As long as a Hot Cross Buns baked on Good Friday remains fresh the men of the house are safe from drowning.

f) Water dipped on Good Friday before sunrise without a word being spoken has healing power and will stay pure all the year.

g) Country folk believed it was a good day to move bees, plant potatoes or prune roses.

h) Three Good Friday loaves pushed into a heap of corn were believed to protect it from rats, mice and weevils.

i) Eggs laid on Good Friday and eaten on that day brought good luck.

So from this far from exhaustive list it is possible to see how the events of Easter have influenced the lives of countless people down the ages whether they were practising Christians or not.

Interesting Facts

1. The name Gethsemane means the oil-press and it was based near the Mount of Olives.

2. In Germany chocolate hares are sometimes given in place of Easter Eggs. Because it is full of energy in the Spring the hare was said to be the favourite animal of the ancient goddess Eastre - the goddess of life and birth.

3. Some people like to think that the Good in Good Friday is good because without it there would have been no Easter.

4. Very few people bear the surname Easter. It was originally a nickname for someone who was connected with the festival such as being born or baptised at that time.

5. The name Good Friday probably came from God's Friday in the same way as goodbye came from God be with ye.

The Ladies of Biddenden, Kent

Mary and Eliza Chaulkhurst of Biddenden, Kent deserve a special mention. They were born joined at the hips and shoulders in 1100. Today we would refer to them as Siamese twins but this term was not used until much later.

They must have been comparatively well off because they were able to leave twenty acres of land to the village for charitable purposes. (It is still known as Bread and Cheese Land.)

On Easter Sunday, after the morning service, 600 so-called cakes are given away to anyone who applies for them. In reality, they are hard biscuits bearing the impression of the two sisters. In addition, the poor of the village receive bread and cheese.

How wonderful to be remembered not for your disability but for your thoughtful kindness.

The Hare and The Easter Bunny

Because the rabbit was capable of having several litters a year it was thought of as a symbol of fertility long before the Christian era. It seems to have become confused with the Easter Hare. The Easter Bunny has no special religious significance of its own.

The association of the hare with the Easter season appears to have originated in Egypt where its name means open or opener. It is a credible Christian symbol. Like Our Lord it has no home.

It is born with its eyes open and is never known to harm other animals. Being a herbivore it does not need to kill for food and it will even help its own kind out of danger.

The golden pelt is said to be invisible in the early morning sun so as the supposed Easter egg bringer it is safe from detection, or so it was believed.

In some countries children are still sent out on Easter Sunday morning to search for the chocolate or dyed decorated eggs the Hare has hidden in the garden.

In some parts of Germany, pretty little moss gardens are prepared so that there will be a safe place for the much prized eggs. Maybe there is a connection between the searching for eggs and the women searching the empty tomb for the body of Jesus.

Some followers of Buddha will have heard the legend that he once transformed himself into a hare so that he could be eaten by a hungry traveller he had found by the roadside. His reward was to be sent to the moon to live for ever in the light.

There is an undeniable charm about these stories which have persisted down the centuries.

Heaving or Lifting

From London to Lancashire and beyond, for many centuries men heaved the women on Easter Monday and the women took their revenge on Easter Tuesday. The custom persisted up to the latter part of the nineteenth century. It seems to have been most popular from Derbyshire northwards.

One account describes how the lifting took place between nine o'clock in the morning and noon. A chair was often provided and it would be decorated with ribbons and favours. It was lifted from the ground three times and turned round at the same time. Then the occupant was kissed by everyone involved in the lifting. He or she was expected to pay a fee to regain their freedom. In some villages the chair was made with the hands.

One record appears to confirm that Edward I was lifted on Easter Monday by the ladies of his Court who then extracted a payment of fourteen pounds to set him free. This was a large sum in those days.

It is believed that the custom was intended to represent the Resurrection of Christ from the dead.

How good it is to realise that behind all the fun and jollity there was the leaven of remembrance.

Riddle-me-ree

My first is in butter but not in fat
My second's in talking and also in chat
My third is in song but not in hymn
My fourth is in bright but not in dim
My fifth is in poem and also in rhyme
My sixth is in dirt and also in grime
My seventh the same as the first, don't you know
My eighth, ninth are twins they're both found in go
My whole is a treat that all may enjoy
Grandparents, parents and each girl and boy.

Answer - ***EASTER EGG.***

Names

Some people collect interesting names for a hobby. Indeed, George Hubbard of New York is reputed to have been delighted when he found someone actually called Luscious Easter.

Interesting too are the derivations of names connected with the Easter Events.

THOMAS comes from Aramaic and means 'the twin'. Before the Norman Conquest it was known in England only as a priest's name but after 1066 it soon came into general use.

JOHN is the English form of Johannes meaning God is gracious. By the end of the sixteenth century it was one of the most common boys' names in the English-speaking world.

JESUS comes from the Hebrew meaning 'Jehovah is generous' or the more popular 'Jehovah saves'.

JUDAS from the Hebrew is believed to have meant 'praise' but is now mostly used as a synonym for 'traitor'.

PETER comes from the Greek 'petros' meaning a stone or 'petra' a rock. It has remained popular down the centuries.

This is an introduction to the study of biblical names. Why not continue it for yourself?

Here is a list of the disciples to start you off. Simon Peter, Andrew, James, John, Philip, Bartholomew, Matthew, Thomas, James(2), Simon, Judas and Judas Iscariot.

Friday the Thirteenth

It is considered unlucky because -

1. Thirteen people sat down to the Last Supper.
2. Jesus was crucified on a Friday.
3. Eve is supposed to have eaten the apple in the Garden of Eden on a Friday.

The Gift of Sight

"Take me with you, please," John Mark begged.

"Not this time," replied Ramah.

"No," said Jera. *"We don't mind usually, but we can't have you today. There'll be lots and lots of people, and, as you can't see, you might lose yourself. If we're to get close to Jesus, we can't have you to hinder us."*

"I understand," said John Mark, trying to stop his lips from trembling. Because he was blind, he missed so many pleasures.

When Emperor Caesar Augustus had passed through the region, John Mark's mother had kept him at home. It was the same when the King of Judea paid the area a visit. John Mark had missed all the excitement. But this Jesus, about whom everybody was talking, seemed to him to be far more important than any emperor or king. Yet he was not to be allowed to join the crowds to cheer his passing.

He could hear his friends, Ramah and Jera, scurrying off down the stony track that led to the Jerusalem road, and he caught the words of Jera as he cried, *"We'll take Him a wonderful present."* But John Mark did not hear what the present might be.

He felt a hand upon his shoulder and he knew at once that it was his mother's. He could not see the gentle sadness in her eyes as she said, *"You are better here, John. The crowded streets of the city are no place for you. In their excitement the people might trample on you. Besides,"* she added softly, *"if you went you wouldn't be able to see our Lord."*

John Mark made no reply. His mother, of course, was right. He would not be able to see Jesus, but if only he could have got near to Him - why, anything might happen. What was it Ramah had said? *"He heals people. He makes the lame to walk and the deaf to hear. They even say that he has raised the dead."*

A plan began to form in John Mark's mind. When his mother left the house to return the washing she took in to earn their food, he would slip away. It might take him a long time to reach the road along which Jesus was to pass, but it was something he could manage despite his lack of sight. He had long known the art of listening to sounds from people and being guided by them.

First, however, he would make a Crown of Flowers for Jesus. That would be his present. Everybody said he had a special way with flowers. His fingers were so sensitive that, even though he could not see the flowers, he could weave them into beautiful shapes. In fact, he had once made a Cross of Flowers for the Temple, and everyone had said how well he had made it.

He knew just where the golden Easter lilies grew - underneath the palm trees higher up the hillside outside his village. He must hurry for he had no time to waste.

As his mother watched him go she was thankful that he seemed to have forgotten his disappointment. She could not blame Ramah and Jera for refusing to take John with them. After all, they were usually very kind to him. And, like all boys, they had gone off long before the proper time. The Christ was said to be resting on His way somewhere before beginning His triumphant journey into Jerusalem. And John would be happy in the Flower Grove. The soft petals of the perfumed blossoms always seemed to give him pleasure.

She might not have been so content had she seen John Mark climbing a palm tree to break off three fine branches. Quickly weaving them into the form of a cross, he set about gathering a bunch of flowers. His hands were so deft that not a petal was bruised, and he hummed happily to himself as he thought, *"If I make the Flower Crown beautiful enough surely the people will let me through to present it to Jesus. And I am sure He would be glad of some sweet-smelling blossoms. It's so hot and sticky riding in this heat."*

Skilfully he mustered the stems until he had formed the flowers into a great golden crown. He intended to fasten the crown to the palm leaf cross. In that way he need not carry it in his hot hands and so cause the flowers to begin to wither.

Hearing a movement beside him, he paused.

"What are you doing, son?" said a deep, yet gentle voice.

"Making a crown, sir."

"And whom do you wish to crown?"

"Jesus of Nazareth. Perhaps you could tell me if he has been

seen yet. I'm so afraid of missing Him. They say He is going to be our earthly king, and I thought the gift of a crown of flowers would show Him I am glad He is to be our ruler."

"A crown of flowers," said the stranger thoughtfully.

"Yes. You see, sir, we are only poor. My mother is a widow, and I could not buy anything for Jesus. And they do say that I make beautiful things with flowers, although, of course, I cannot see them."

"You may be sure that this crown is very beautiful."

"I'm so glad," said John Mark. "If Jesus is very tired He might like to feel the petals on his forehead. They would be cool and refreshing."

"They would indeed, son. Tell me, what is your name?"

"John Mark."

"A strong name," said the stranger. "Is it your greatest wish to see this Jesus?"

"Oh, yes. I wish that more than anything else."

"Why?"

"Because I would like to serve Him. But first I must meet Him."

"You *have* met Him. John Mark, come here."

The boy obeyed. He felt a light touch on his eyelids and suddenly the darkness diminished and vanished. With a thrill of delight, John Mark blinked unbelievingly. He placed his hands before his eyes and then took them away.

"I can see!" he shouted. "I can see!"

He looked in growing wonder at the blue of the sky and the green of the grass. He was taking in the miracle of the hills when he remembered the One who had given him sight. He looked along the track, to see Him going quickly down the roadway. At a bend in the path He turned and waved to the boy. And John Mark felt a wonderful thrill when he saw that in His hand was a palm leaf cross and on His brow a crown of golden flowers.

"It was Jesus!" John Mark whispered, "And He has accepted my gift." _____

The Lesson. If we live to give, anything we gain is an unexpected bonus.

MOORLEY'S

are growing Publishers, adding several new titles to our list each year. We also undertake private publications and commissioned works.

Our range of publications includes: **Books of Verse**
Devotional Poetry
Recitations
Drama
Bible Plays
Sketches
Nativity Plays
Passiontide Plays
Easter Plays
Demonstrations
Resource Books
Assembly Material
Songs & Musicals
Children's Addresses
Prayers & Graces
Daily Readings
Books for Speakers
Activity Books
Quizzes
Puzzles
Painting Books
Daily Readings
Church Stationery
Notice Books
Cradle Rolls
Hymn Board Numbers

Please send a S.A.E. (approx 9" x 6") for the current catalogue or consult your local Christian Bookshop who should stock or be able to order our titles.